The 30th
Anniversary
Concert Celebration

BOB DYLAN

The 30th Anniversary Concert Celebration

The 30th Anniversary Concert Celebration

The 30th Anniversary Concert Celebration

The 30th Anniversary Concert Celebration

The 30th Anniversary Concert Celebration

Cover art direction: Chris Austopchuk
Assistance: Jim de Barros
Computer graphics: Richard O. White
Photography: Ken Regan

Order No. AM 91474
US International Standard Book Number: 0.8256.1375.2
UK International Standard Book Number: 0.7119.3711.7

Exclusive Distributors:
Music Sales Corporation
257 Park Avenue South, New York, NY 10010
Music Sales Limited
8/9 Frith Street, London W1V 5TZ England
Music Sales Pty. Limited
120 Rothschild Street, Rosebery, Sydney, NSW 2018, Australia

Printed in the United States of America by
Vicks Lithograph and Printing Corporation

CONTENTS

In the end, it was about the songs.

On October 16, 1992, an impressive and eclectic group of artists gathered at Madison Square Garden in New York City for the purpose of celebrating the music of Bob Dylan on the occasion of his 30th anniversary of recording. Bringing together musical greats as far-flung as Johnny Cash and Eddie Vedder, The Clancy Brothers and Lou Reed, the four-hour show celebrated a truly remarkable lifetime of songs in front of a sold-out audience of over 18,000. Warmly dubbed the Bobfest by participant Neil Young, the show was broadcast around the world and featured a cast of musical notables performing carefully chosen and often surprising selections from the incomparable Dylan songbook. At evening's end, the man of honor himself appeared on stage and gracefully brought it all back home again. In a world where all-star celebrity gatherings have become commonplace, the Bob Dylan celebration stood out as, first and foremost, a legitimately memorable musical event.

John Mellencamp, who's been covering "Like A Rolling Stone" in concert for years, bravely took on the Dylan classic early in the show and delivered a fairly faithful and altogether convincing cover featuring strong vocal help from Pat Peterson and Sue Medley. Joining Mellencamp and his excellent band for the event on organ was Al Kooper, reprising his prominent part from Dylan's 1965 original, which was voted the best single of the last 25 years by *Rolling Stone* in 1988. Mellencamp—who's been instrumental in the activities of Farm Aid, which Dylan helped inspire with his onstage comments at Live Aid, and who directed Dylan's "Political World" video in 1989—was also in fine form for a rousing, bluesy "Leopard-Skin Pill-Box Hat" from 1966's *Blonde On Blonde*.

One of the obvious emotional highlights of the show was Stevie Wonder's endlessly soulful rendition of "Blowin' In The Wind," a song Wonder brought to the Top Ten of the Pop and R&B charts back in 1966, three years after Peter, Paul & Mary first introduced it to the masses. As Wonder pointed out in his moving introduction, the message of "Blowin' In The Wind" remains, sadly, one of enduring relevance. A contemporary folk standard originally recorded for 1962's *The Freewheelin' Bob Dylan*, the song found Wonder working his gospel-tinged magic alongside Booker T. Jones and the M.G.'s—the phenomenally adept house band for the show.

Booker T. & The M.G.'s now features Jones on organ, Steve Cropper on guitar, Donald "Duck" Dunn on bass and Anton Fig, filling in for the late Al Jackson, on drums. The group enjoyed a run of instrumental hits in the sixties, including "Green Onions" and "Time Is Tight," as well as serving as the legendary house band for countless Stax classics. The very able musical director of the show was G.E. Smith, longtime *Saturday Night Live* band leader and veteran Dylan guitarist. Also making a significant contribution to the proceedings was session drumming great Jim Keltner, who's worked with the Traveling Wilburys and just about everyone else over the years.

In a winning example of one ingenious lyricist honoring another, Lou Reed righteously rocked out on "Foot Of Pride," an obscure outtake from the 1983 *Infidels* album that Reed, like so many other less famous Bob Dylan fans, discovered on 1991's *The Bootleg Series (Vols. I–III)* set. Hardly an obvious song choice, Reed's "Foot Of Pride" was gutsy as well as a hard-rocking reminder of just how much depth there is to Bob Dylan's body of work.

The riveting acoustic rendition of "Masters Of War," by Pearl Jam's Eddie Vedder and Mike McCready, was arguably the evening's most pleasant surprise. These two young Dylan fans didn't need any loud Seattle sonics to get across Dylan's pointed protest classic from *The Freewheelin' Bob Dylan*. Vedder, who blissfully watched rehearsals for the concert from the front row of a nearly empty Madison Square Garden, proved with his wonderfully intense interpretation that when it comes to a great song, there's no such thing as a generation gap.

Tracy Chapman—who helped bring folk music back to the forefront with her acclaimed 1988 debut album, and who has toured with Dylan occasionally in recent years—offered an eloquent and moving acoustic solo version of the oft-covered "The Times They Are A-Changin'," the title track of Dylan's 1964 effort. In Chapman's capable hands, the song's power remains undimmed by time.

Country and rockabilly legend Johnny Cash and Bob Dylan have a long history of mutual admiration for one another. They first met at the Newport Folk Festival in 1964, and went on to record a session together in Nashville in 1969. The normally T.V.-shy Dylan even appeared on a Cash television special taped at the Grand Ole Opry in 1969. Cash and Dylan's duet on "Girl Of The North Country" was featured on Dylan's groundbreaking country-rock effort *Nashville Skyline*, for which Cash wrote the Grammy Award-winning liner notes. At the show, Cash and June Carter Cash, his wife and longtime musical partner, teamed up for a surprisingly celebratory, down-home version of "It Ain't Me, Babe," a song from *Another Side Of Bob Dylan* that Cash took up the charts in 1964, well before the Turtles turned it into a pop smash in 1965.

Willie Nelson and Bob Dylan are clearly two kindred spirits. Recently the pair collaborated on "Heartland" from Nelson's new *Across The Borderline* album, which also included a cover of Dylan's "What Was It You Wanted"—a standout track from 1989's *Oh Mercy* that Nelson performed for the first time at the event. Playing bass on this swampy and sly rendition was Don Was, who produced *Across The Borderline* as well as co-producing Dylan's 1990 effort *Under The Red Sky*.

Nelson and Was stuck around to back up Kris Kristofferson for his appropriately mellow version of "I'll Be Your Baby Tonight," the song from Dylan's 1968 album *John Wesley Harding*. Kristofferson—one of the many gifted and literate young singer-songwriters of the sixties and seventies who faced daunting critical comparisons to Dylan—became friendly with Dylan on the set of Sam Peckinpaw's 1973 western film *Pat Garrett And Billy The Kid*, in which they both appeared. Even earlier, however, Kristofferson worked as the studio janitor during the famed *Blonde On Blonde* sessions.

A monumental display of blues power came from veteran Texas guitar hero Johnny Winter, who threw down a furious deep-blues take on "Highway 61 Revisited," which Winter first cut on his 1970 three-sided sophomore Columbia release, *Second Winter*. The guitar line-up of Winter, Steve Cropper and G.E. Smith was in fierce form for the song, living up to the spirit of the late Mike Bloomfield's riffing on Dylan's 1965 original.

Ron Wood's barn-burning version of "Seven Days" provided another of the evening's most happy surprises. An unreleased rocker performed live by Dylan on 1976's "Rolling Thunder Review," the song was subsequently recorded by Wood for his 1979 album *Gimme Some Neck*. With Heartbreaker Howie Epstein joining the house band on bass, the Stone alone, who has often played and recorded with Dylan over the years, came through with a great throaty vocal that was more than a little reminiscent of the song's writer.

Richie Havens, who in his early days played many of the same Greenwich Village folk haunts as Dylan, first cut "Just Like A Woman" for his *Mixed Bag* album back in 1967. He's subsequently recorded and performed numerous Dylan songs, some of which can be heard on his 1987 collection *Richie Havens Sings The Beatles And Dylan*. His solo acoustic version of the song at the celebration was a powerful testament to his abilities as a distinctive interpretative singer.

Arguably the foremost Irish folk singers in the world, The Clancy Brothers from Carrick-On-Suir in the county Tipperary were already a famous group during Dylan's early folkie days. For the Dylan show, they were joined by their longtime musical associate and special guest Tommy Makem as well as their nephew Robbie O'Connell for a haunting traditional take on "When The Ship Comes In," a stirring ballad which first appeared on *The Times They Are A-Changin'* album. The Brothers flew in from Ireland specifically to play the show.

Rosanne Cash, Mary-Chapin Carpenter and Shawn Colvin—a trio of the most gifted women singer-songwriters around and major Bob fans all—teamed up to trade off verses for a gorgeous, harmony-drenched cover of "You Ain't Goin' Nowhere," a *Basement Tapes* gem that was rerecorded by Dylan with Happy Traum for 1972's *Bob Dylan's Greatest Hits Vol. II* set, as well as being a standout cut on The Byrds' 1968 classic *Sweethearts Of The Rodeo* album.

Another kindred spirit and inspired party guest who turned in a great performance at the celebration was Neil Young, who somehow transformed The M.G.'s and drumming ace Jim Keltner into a fantastically loose, Crazy Horse-styled outfit for a strong reading of "Just Like Tom Thumb's Blues" from *Highway 61 Revisited*, and an extended, fiery version of "All Along The Watchtower" that borrowed some its kinetic power from Jimi Hendrix's famed reworking of the *John Wesley Harding* song.

Everyone from Sting to Bette Midler to the Heptones has covered "I Shall Be Released," but Chrissie Hynde, the gifted Pretenders auteur, managed to make the song her own with a radiant performance at the Dylan event, featuring some prominent keyboard assistance from Paul Shaffer. The song was part of the famed *Basement Tapes*, written and casually recorded with The Band at Big Pink in Woodstock in 1967, and subsequently recorded by The Band for its extraordinary 1968 debut album.

The traditionally show-stopping Eric Clapton, who performed a duet with Dylan on "Sign Language" from his *No Reason To Cry* album in 1976, came through with a startling and moving performance at the celebration. The highlight of his set—which also included a luminous "Love Minus Zero, No Limit"—was a truly revelatory rendition of "Don't Think Twice, It's All Right," from *The Freewheelin' Bob Dylan*, that Clapton and Booker T. Jones radically rearranged into a seductive new bluesy masterpiece, complete with some incendiary soloing from the guitar master himself.

Famed for such seventies soul smashes as "Back Stabbers," "Love Train" and "For The Love Of Money," The O'Jays had a Top Five R&B hit with "Emotionally Yours," a delicate love song from 1985's *Empire Burlesque* that the group recorded in two completely different arrangements on its 1990 *Emotionally Yours* album. Backed by a gospel choir featuring the great Cissy Houston, The O'Jays brought a churchly spirit to the festivities with their stately version of the song.

The history of The Band is, of course, inextricably tied to that of Bob Dylan. It was only fitting, then, that the current incarnation of The Band—featuring original members Levon Helm, Rick Danko and Garth Hudson—came together for a fine loose-grooving version of "When I Paint My Masterpiece." The song was originally recorded with Leon Russell on piano in 1971 for *Bob Dylan's Greatest Hits Vol. II*, the same year that it became a highlight of The Band's album *Cahoots*.

A fellow Traveling Wilbury and longtime friend, George Harrison goes way back with Dylan. Before their prominent Wilbury collaboration, Dylan and the then newly former Beatle co-wrote "I'd Have You Anytime" for Harrison's *All Things Must Pass*, the 1970 album for which Harrison also recorded a version of Dylan's "If Not For You." For the celebration, Harrison returned to Madison Square Garden, site of the 1971 Concerts for Bangladesh, and utterly charmed the crowd by delivering an exquisite, clearly loving rendition of "Absolutely Sweet Marie" from *Blonde On Blonde*.

Tom Petty (another wildly talented Wilbury brother in good standing) and the eternally impressive Heartbreakers recorded and toured the world extensively with Dylan for a period during the mid-eighties. At the Dylan event, Petty & The Heartbreakers—guitarist Mike Campbell, keyboardist Benmont Tench, bassist Howie Epstein and drummer Stan Lynch—were in peak form, offering a totally inspired and subtle reading of "License To Kill," an underappreciated number from Dylan's 1983 *Infidels* album. Switching gears brilliantly, they tore into a wild, rollicking rave-up performance of "Rainy Day Women #12 & 35," from the *Blonde On Blonde* album, that brought the house down.

Roger McGuinn, founder of The Byrds, has been a major interpreter of Dylan's material over the years. In 1965, he and other Byrds transformed Dylan's "Mr. Tambourine Man" into a global smash, and went on to record many other Dylan compositions, including "All I Really Want To Do," "You Ain't Goin' Nowhere," "My Back Pages" and "Chimes Of Freedom." Joined by Tom Petty & The Heartbreakers, McGuinn and his Rickenbacker let "Mr. Tambourine Man" ring out wonderfully one more time.

As for the man of honor himself, Dylan began his own set with "Song To Woody," a moving composition from his debut album that remains a gracious salute to Dylan's own early influence, Woody Guthrie. Unfortunately, technical problems prevent the song's inclusion here. Dylan followed with a wonderfully intense rendition of "It's Alright, Ma (I'm Only Bleeding)" from *Bringing It All Back Home*, that served as a vivid reminder of his incomparable acoustic power. "My Back Pages," originally from 1964's *Another Side Of Bob Dylan*, became a history-making group effort with McGuinn, Petty, Young, Clapton, Dylan and Harrison all trading off on the classic verses. Then "Knockin' On Heaven's Door"—the elegiac standard from the *Pat Garrett And Billy The Kid* soundtrack recently covered by Guns N' Roses—brought all the evening's players out for a memorable ensemble encore.

Finally, after the television satellite feed was shut down, Bob Dylan generously returned to the stage for a lovely, understated version of "Girl Of The North Country" that proved one more time what one man can do armed with only his voice, guitar and extraordinary songs.

—David Wild

Like A Rolling Stone

Words and Music by Bob Dylan

Verse 2. You've gone to the finest school all right Miss Lonely,
But you know you only used to get
Juiced in it.
And nobody's ever taught you how to live on the street
And now you're gonna have to get
Used to it.
You said you'd never compromise
With the mystery tramp, but now you realize
He's not selling any alibis
As you stare into the vacuum of his eyes
And ask him do you want to
Make a deal?

Refrain:

Verse 3. You never turned around to see the frowns on the jugglers and the clowns
When they all come down
And did tricks for you
You never understood that it ain't no good
You shouldn't let other people
Get your kicks for you.
You used to ride on the chrome horse with your diplomat
Who carried on his shoulder a Siamese cat,
Ain't it hard when you discovered that
He really wasn't where it's at
After he took from you everything
He could steal.

Refrain:

Verse 4. Princess on the steeple
And all the pretty people're drinkin', thinkin'
That they got it made.
Exchanging all kinds of precious gifts and things
But you'd better lift your diamond ring,
You'd better pawn it babe,
You used to be so amused
At Napoleon in rags and the language that he used
Go to him now, he calls you, you can't refuse
When you got nothing,you got nothing to lose,
You're invisible now, you got no secrets
To conceal.

Refrain:

Leopard-Skin Pill-Box Hat

Words and Music by Bob Dylan

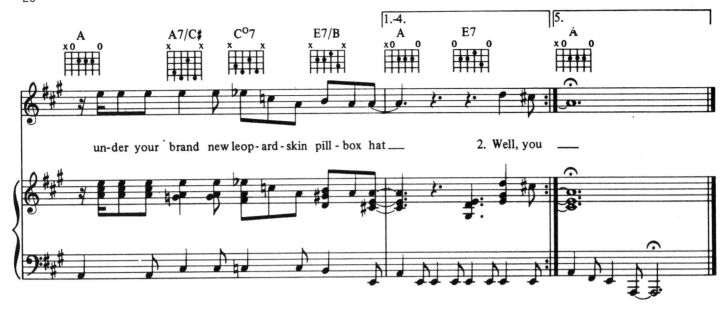

un-der your brand new leop-ard-skin pill-box hat___   2. Well, you ___

Additional Lyrics

2. Well, you look so pretty in it
   Honey, can I jump on it sometime?
   Yes, I just wanna see
   If it's really that expensive kind
   You know it balances on your head
   Just like a mattress balances
   On a bottle of wine
   Your brand new leopard-skin pill-box hat

3. Well, if you wanna see the sun rise
   Honey, I know where
   We'll go out and see it sometime
   We'll both just sit there and stare
   Me with my belt
   Wrapped around my head
   And you just sittin' there
   In your brand new leopard-skin pill-box hat

4. Well, I asked the doctor if I could see you
   It's bad for your health, he said
   Yes, I disobeyed his orders
   I came to see you
   But I found him there instead
   You know, I don't mind him cheatin' on me
   But I sure wish he'd take that off his head
   Your brand new leopard-skin pill-box hat

5. Well, I see you got a new boyfriend
   You know, I never seen him before
   Well, I saw him
   Makin' love to you
   You forgot to close the garage door
   You might think he loves you for your money
   But I know what he really loves you for
   It's your brand new leopard-skin pill-box hat

Blowin' In The Wind

Words and Music by Bob Dylan

1. How man-y roads must a man walk___ down be-fore you call him a man? Yes, 'n' How man-y
2. How man-y times must a man look___ up be-fore he can see___ the sky? Yes, 'n' how man-y

friend, is blow-in' in the wind, The an - swer is

blow-in' in the wind.

Additional Lyrics

3. How many years can a mountain exist
before it is washed to the sea?
Yes 'n' how many years can some people exist
before they're allowed to be free?
Yes 'n' how many times can a man turn his head
pretending that he just doesn't see?

The answer, my friend, is blowin' in the wind,
The answer is blowin' in the wind.

Foot Of Pride

Words and Music by Bob Dylan

Additional lyrics

2. Hear ya got a brother named James, don't forget faces or names.
   Sunken cheeks and his blood is mixed,
   He looked straight into the sun and said, "revenge is mine."
   But he drinks, and drinks can be fixed.
   Sing me one more song, about ya love me to the moon and the stranger,
   And your fall by the sword love affair with Eroll Flynn.
   In these times of compassion when conformity's in fashion,
   Say one more stupid thing to me before the final nail is driven in.

   (Chorus)

3. There's a retired businessman named Red, cast down from heaven and he's out of his head.
   He feeds off of everyone that he can touch,
   He said he only deals in cash or sells tickets to a plane crash.
   He's not somebody that you play around with much.
   Miss Delilah is his, a philistine is what she is.
   She'll do wondrous works with your fate,
   Feed you coconut bread, spice buns in your bed,
   If you don't mind sleepin' with your head face down in a grave.

   (Chorus)

4. Well, they'll choose a man for you to meet tonight.
   You'll play the fool and learn how to walk through doors,
   How to enter into the gates of paradise.
   No, how to carry a burden too heavy to be yours.
   Yeah, from the stage they'll be tryin' to get water outta rocks.
   A whore will pass the hat, collect a hundred grand and say, "thanks."
   They like to take all this money from sin, build big universities to study in,
   Sing "Amazing Grace" all the way to the Swiss banks.

   (Chorus)

5. They got some beautiful people out there, man.
   They can be a terror to your mind and show you how to hold your tongue.
   They got mystery written all over their forehead.
   They kill babies in the crib and say only the good die young.
   They don't believe in mercy.
   Judgment on them is something that you'll never see.
   They can exalt you up or bring you down main route,
   Turn you into anything that they want you to be.

   (Chorus)

6. Yes, I guess I loved him too,
   I can still see him in my mind climbin' that hill.
   Did he make it to the top? Well, he probably did and dropped,
   Struck down by the strength of the will.
   Ain't nothin' left here, partner, just the dust of a plague that has left this whole town afraid.
   From now on, this'll be where you're from.
   Let the dead bury the dead. Your time will come.
   Let hot iron blow as he raised the shade.

   (Chorus to instrumental fade)

The 30th Aniversary Concert Celebration

Masters Of War

Words and Music by Bob Dylan

walls   You that hide be-hind desks   I just

want you to know I can see through your masks

D.S. %

2. You that never done nothin'
   But build to destroy
   You play with my world
   Like it's your little toy
   You put a gun in my hand
   And you hide from my eyes
   And you turn and run farther
   When the fast bullets fly

3. Like Judas of old
   You lie and deceive
   A world war can be won
   You want me to believe
   But I see through your eyes
   And I see through your brain
   Like I see through the water
   That runs down my drain

4. You fasten the triggers
   For the others to fire
   Then you set back and watch
   When the death count gets higher
   You hide in your mansion
   As young people's blood
   Flows out of their bodies
   And is buried in the mud

5. You've thrown the worst fear
   That can ever be hurled
   Fear to bring children
   Into the world
   For threatenin' my baby
   Unborn and unnamed
   You ain't worth the blood
   That runs in your veins

6. How much do I know
   To talk out of turn
   You might say that I'm young
   You might say I'm unlearned
   But there's one thing I know
   Though I'm younger than you
   Even Jesus would never
   Forgive what you do

7. Let me ask you one question
   Is your money that good
   Will it buy you forgiveness
   Do you think that it could
   I think you will find
   When your death takes its toll
   All the money you made
   Will never buy back your soul

8. And I hope that you die
   And your death'll come soon
   I will follow your casket
   On a pale afternoon
   And I'll watch while you're lowered
   Down to your death bed
   And I'll stand o'er your grave
   Till I'm sure that you're dead.

The Times They Are A-Changin'

Words and Music by Bob Dylan

2. Come writers and critics
   Who prophecies with your pen
   And keep your eyes wide
   The chance won't come again.
   And don't speak too soon
   For the wheel's still in spin
   And there's no tellin' who
   That it's namin'
   For the loser now
   Will be later to win
   For the times they are a-changin'.

3. Come senators, congressmen
   Please heed the call
   Don't stand in the doorway
   Don't block up the hall.
   For he that gets hurt
   Will be he who has stalled
   There's a battle
   Outside and it's ragin'
   It'll soon shake your windows
   And rattle your walls
   For the times they are a-changin'.

4. Come mothers and fathers,
   Throughout the land
   And don't criticize
   What you can't understand.
   Your sons and your daughters
   Are beyond your command
   Your old road is
   Rapidly agin'
   Please get out of the new one
   If you can't lend your hand
   For the times they are a-changin'.

5. The line it is drawn
   The curse it is cast
   The slow one now will
   Later be fast.
   As the present now
   Will later be past
   The order is rapidly fadin'
   And the first one now
   Will later be last
   For the times they are a-changin'.

It Ain't Me, Babe

Words and Music by Bob Dylan

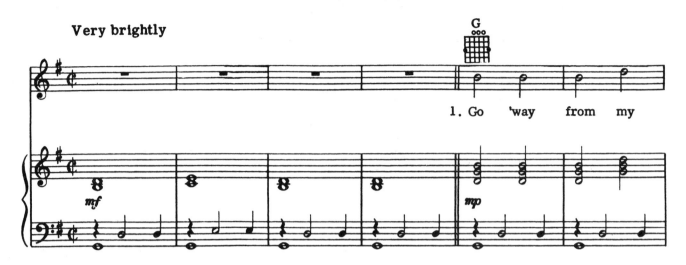

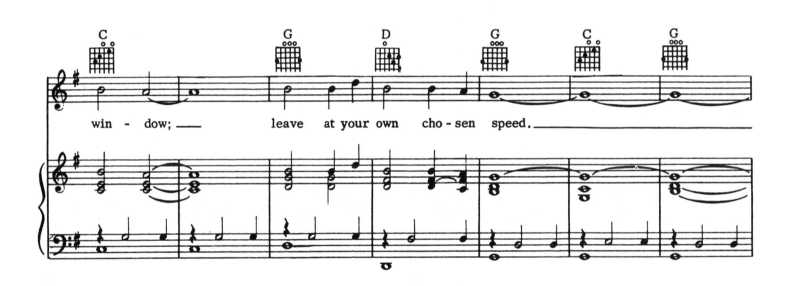

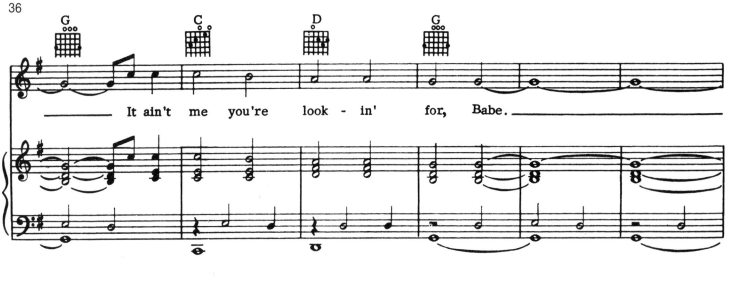

It ain't me you're look-in' for, Babe.

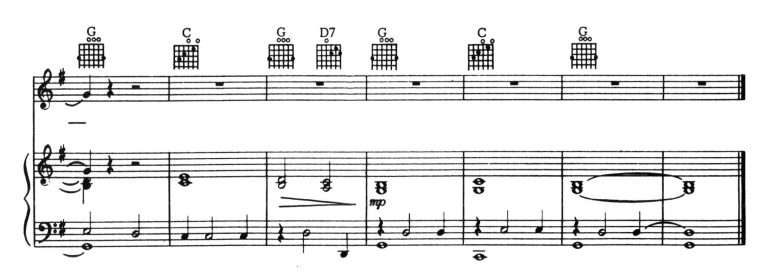

2. Go lightly from the ledge Babe,
   Go lightly on the ground,
   I'm not the one you want, Babe,
   I will only let you down.
   You say you're looking for someone
   Who will promise never to part,
   Someone to close his eyes for you,
   Someone to close his heart.
   Someone who will die for you an' more
   But it ain't me, Babe,
   No, no, no it ain't me, Babe,
   It ain't me you're looking for, Babe.

3. Go melt back into the nite Babe,
   Everything inside is made of stone,
   There's nothing in here moving
   An' anyway I'm not alone.
   You say you're looking for someone
   Who'll pick you up each time you fall,
   To gather flowers constantly
   An' to come each time you call.
   A lover for your life an' nothing more
   But it ain't me, Babe,
   No, no, no it ain't me, Babe,
   It ain't me you're looking for, Babe.

What Was It You Wanted

Words and Music by Bob Dylan

Slow, with a steady beat

I'll Be Your Baby Tonight

Words and Music by Bob Dylan

48

shoes off,— Do not fear,— Bring that bot-

-tle o-ver here,—

I'll _____ be your _____ ba-by to-

night. _____

Highway 61 Revisited

Words and Music by Bob Dylan

1. Oh God said to A-bra-ham kill me a son Abe says man you must be put-tin' me on __ God say no Abe say what

Repeat 4 times

2. Well Georgia Sam he had a bloody nose
   Welfare Department they wouldn't give him no clothes
   He asked poor Howard where can I go
   Howard said there's only one place I know
   Sam said tell me quick man I got to run
   Ol' Howard just pointed with his gun
   And said that way down on Highway 61.

3. Well Mack the Finger said to Louie the King
   I got forty red white and blue shoe strings
   And a thousand telephones that don't ring
   Do you know where I can get rid of these things
   And Louie the King said let me think for a minute son
   And he said yes I think it can be easily done
   Just take everything down to Highway 61.

4. Now the fifth daughter on the twelfth night
   Told the first father that things weren't right
   My complexion she said is much too white
   He said come here and step into the light he says hmm you're right
   Let me tell the second mother this has been done
   But the second mother was with the seventh son
   And they were both out on Highway 61.

5. Now the rovin' gambler he was very bored
   He was tryin' to create a next world war
   He found a promoter who nearly fell off the floor
   He said I never engaged in this kind of thing before
   But yes I think it can be very easily done
   We'll just put some bleachers out in the sun
   And have it on Highway 61.

Seven Days

Words and Music by Bob Dylan

The 30th Anniversary Concert Celebration

Just Like A Woman

Words and Music by Bob Dylan

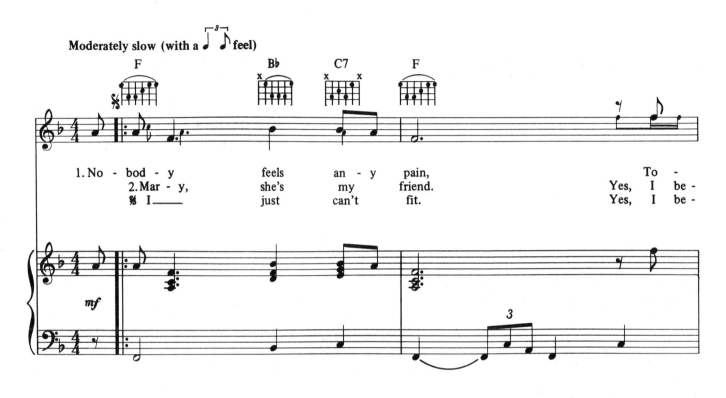

1. No - bod - y   feels   an - y   pain,   To -
2. Mar - y,   she's   my   friend.   Yes, I be -
  I ____   just   can't   fit.   Yes, I be -

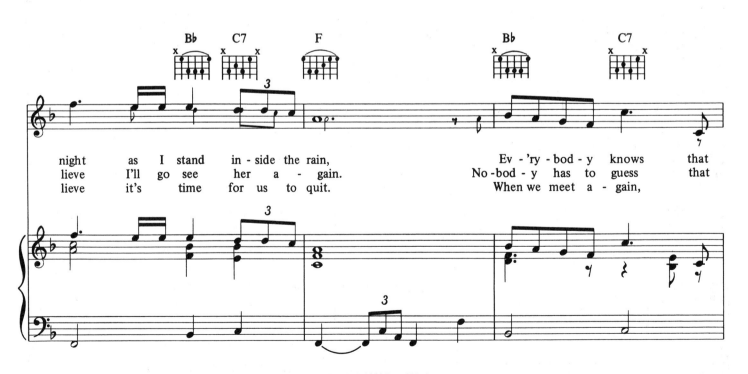

night   as I stand   in - side the rain,   Ev - 'ry - bod - y knows   that
lieve   I'll go see   her a - gain.   No - bod - y has to guess   that
lieve   it's time   for us to quit.   When we meet a - gain,   that

When The Ship Comes In

Words and Music by Bob Dylan

shore-line sands will be shak-ing___ Then the tide will sound And the wind will pound And the

morn-ing will be break - ing. _____

D.S. 3 times 𝄌

2. Oh the fishes will laugh
   As they swim out of the path
   And the seagulls they'll be smiling
   And the rocks on the sand
   Will proudly stand
   The hour that the ship comes in.

   And the words they use
   For to get the ship confused
   Will not be understood as they're spoken
   For the chains of the sea
   Will have busted in the night
   And will be buried at the bottom of the ocean.

3. A song will lift
   As the mainsail shifts
   And the boat drifts on to the shore line
   And the sun will respect
   Every face on the deck
   The hour when the ship comes in.

   Then the sands will roll
   Out a carpet of gold
   For your weary toes to be a touchin'
   And the ship's wise men
   Will remind you once again
   That the whole wide world is watchin'.

4. Oh the foes will rise
   With the sleep still in their eyes
   And they'll jerk from their beds and think they're dreamin'
   But they'll pinch themselves and squeal
   And know that it's for real
   The hour when the ship comes in.

   Then they'll raise their hands
   Sayin' we'll meet all your demands
   But we'll shout from the bow your days are numbered
   And like Pharoah's triumph
   They'll be drownded in the tide
   And like Goliath they'll be conquered.

You Ain't Goin' Nowhere

Words and Music by Bob Dylan

Just Like Tom Thumb's Blues

Words and Music by Bob Dylan

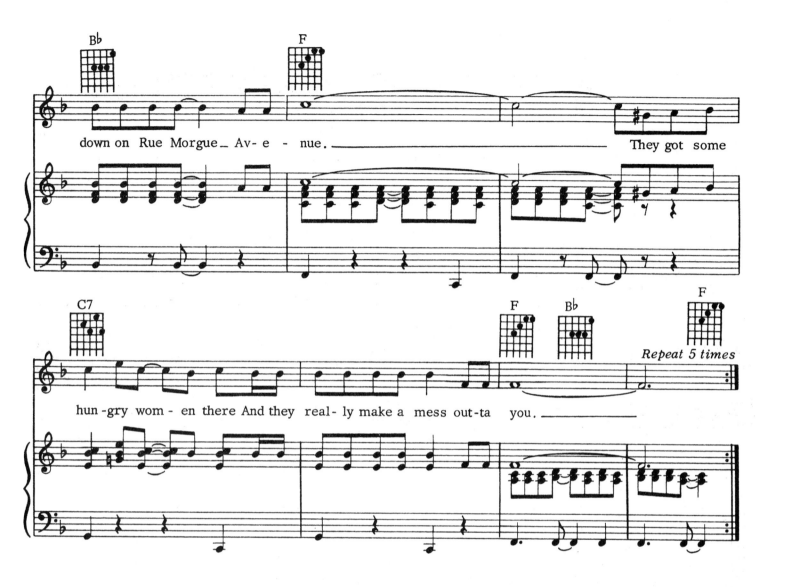

2. Now if you see Saint Annie
   Please tell her thanks a lot
   I cannot move
   My fingers are all in a knot
   I don't have the strength
   To get up and take another shot
   And my best friend my doctor
   Won't even say what it is I've got

3. Sweet Melinda
   The peasants call her the goddess of gloom
   She speaks good English
   And she invites you up into her room
   And you're so kind
   And careful not to go to her too soon
   And she takes your voice
   And leaves you howling at the moon

4. Up on Housing Project Hill
   It's either fortune or fame
   You must pick up one or the other
   Though neither of them are to be what they claim
   If you're lookin' to get silly
   You better go back to from where you came
   Because the cops don't need you
   And man they expect the same

5. Now all the authorities
   They just stand around and boast
   How they blackmailed the sergeant at arms
   Into leaving his post
   And picking up Angel who
   Just arrived here from the coast
   Who looked so fine at first
   But left looking just like a ghost

6. I started out on burgundy
   But soon hit the harder stuff
   Everybody said they'd stand behind me
   When the game got rough
   But the joke was on me
   There was nobody even there to call my bluff
   I'm going back to New York City
   I do believe I've had enough

All Along The Watchtower

Words and Music by Bob Dylan

I Shall Be Released

Words and Music by Bob Dylan

Additional Lyrics

2. Down here next to me in this lonely crowd
   Is a man who swears he's not to blame.
   All day long I hear him cry so loud,
   Calling out that he's been framed.

   Chorus

3. They say ev'rything can be replaced,
   Yet ev'ry distance is not near.
   So I remember ev'ry face
   Of ev'ry man who put me here.

   Chorus

The 30th Anniversary Concert Celebration

Don't Think Twice, It's All Right

Words and Music by Bob Dylan

Emotionally Yours

Words and Music by Bob Dylan

Come, ba - by, find_ me,
Come, ba - by, rock_ me,

Come, ba - by, re - mind_ me_
Come, ba - by, lock_ me_

of_ where I once be - gun._
in - to the shad - ows of your heart.

When I Paint My Masterpiece

Words and Music by Bob Dylan

Sail - in' 'round the world _____ in a dirt - y gon - do - la.

Oh, to be back _ in the land _ of Co - ca _ Co - la!

D. S. al Coda

I left

dif-f'rent When I paint my mas-ter - piece. _____

rit.

R. H.

Pedal

Absolutely Sweet Marie

Words and Music by Bob Dylan

License To Kill

Words and Music by Bob Dylan

Moderately slow, in 2

Verse
1. Man thinks 'cause he rules the earth, __ he can do with it as __ he please. __

And if things don't change soon, change soon,

he will. __ Oh, __ man has in-vent-ed his doom. __

Verse 2.
```
      ‖G              |Em        |
Now, they take him and they teach him
D              |G
And they groom him for life
      |          |Em                    |D      |
And they set him on a path where he's bound to get ill
      |C        |G
Then they bury him with stars
      |                     |C
Sell his body like they do used cars
```

Chorus II.
```
      ‖Em    C    |Em    C
Now, there's a woman  on my block
      |Em   C       |Em     C
She just sit there  facin' the hill
      |G             |D            |G    Gsus4 |G
She say who gonna take away his license to kill
```

Verse 3.
```
      ‖G              |Em        |
Now, he's hell bent for destruction
D              |G
He's afraid and confused
      |             |Em              |D      |        |
And his brain has been mismanaged with great skill
C             |G
All he believes are his eyes
      |                   |C
And his eyes, they just tell him lies
```

Chorus III.
```
      ‖Em    C    |Em        C
But there's a woman  on my block
      |Em           |Em    C
Sitting there  in a cold chill
      |G             |D            |G    Gsus4 |G        ‖
She say who gonna take away his license to kill
```

Bridge

Verse 4.
```
      ‖G              |Em        |
Now he worships at an altar
D              |G
Of a stagnant pool
      |             |Em                |D      |
And when he sees his reflection, he's fulfilled
      |C                 |G
Oh, man is opposed to fair play
      |                   |C
He wants it all and he wants it his way
```

Chorus I

Rainy Day Women #12 & 35

Words and Music by Bob Dylan

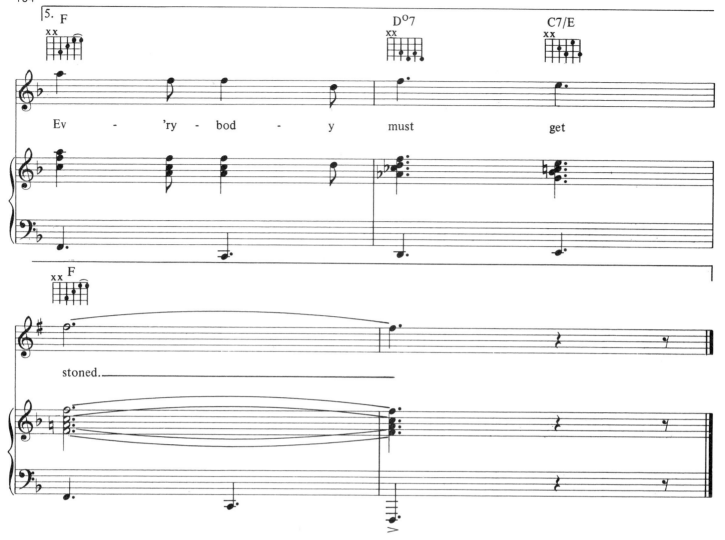

5. F   D°7   C7/E

Ev - 'ry - bod - y   must   get

F

stoned.

Additional Lyrics

2. Well, they'll stone ya when you're walkin' 'long the street.
   They'll stone ya when you're tryin' to keep your seat.
   They'll stone ya when you're walkin' on the floor.
   They'll stone ya when you're walkin' to the door.
   But I would not feel so all alone,
   Everybody must get stoned.

3. They'll stone ya when you're at the breakfast table.
   They'll stone ya when you are young and able.
   They'll stone ya when you're tryin' to make a buck.
   They'll stone ya and then they'll say, "Good luck."
   Tell ya what, I would not feel so all alone,
   Everybody must get stoned.

4. Well, they'll stone you and say that it's the end.
   Then they'll stone you and then they'll come back again.
   They'll stone you when you're riding in your car.
   They'll stone you when you're playing your guitar.
   Yes, but I would not feel so all alone,
   Everybody must get stoned.

5. Well, they'll stone you when you walk all alone.
   They'll stone you when you are walking home.
   They'll stone you and then say you are brave.
   They'll stone you when you are set down in your grave.
   But I would not feel so all alone,
   Everybody must get stoned.

Mr. Tambourine Man

Words and Music by Bob Dylan

5th time Fine

jin-gle jan - gle morn-in' I'll come fol - low-in' you. _____

Verse

1. Though I know that eve-nin's em - pire has re-turned in-to sand,

Van-ished from my hand, Left me blind-ly here to stand but still not

sleep-in'! _____ My wea-ri-ness a - maz-es me I'm

brand - ed on my feet. I have no one to meet And the

an-cient emp-ty street's too dead for dream-in'. _____

Repeat 3 times

Refrain:

Verse 2. Take me on a trip upon your magic swirlin' ship
My senses have been stripped, my hands can't feel to grip
My toes too numb to step, wait only for my boot heels
To be wanderin'
I'm ready to go anywhere, I'm ready for to fade
Into my own parade, cast your dancin' spell my way
I promise to go under it.

Refrain:

Verse 3. Though you might hear laughin' spinnin' swingin' madly across the sun
It's not aimed at anyone, it's just escapin' on the run
And but for the sky there are no fences facin'
And if you hear vague traces of skippin' reels of rhyme
To your tambourine in time, it's just a ragged clown behind
I wouldn't pay it any mind, it's just a shadow you're
Seein' that he's chasin'.

Refrain:

Verse 4. Then take me disappearin' through the smoke rings of my mind
Down the foggy ruins of time, far past the frozen leaves
The haunted, frightened trees out to the windy beach
Far from the twisted reach of crazy sorrow
Yes, to dance beneath the diamond sky with one hand wavin' free
Silhouetted by the sea, circled by the circus sands
With all memory and fate driven deep beneath the waves
Let me forget about today until tomorrow.

Refrain:

It's Alright, Ma (I'm Only Bleeding)

Words and Music by Bob Dylan

ear IT'S AL - RIGHT MA, _____ I'm on - ly sigh-ing.

2. As some warn victory, some downfall
Private reasons great or small
Can be seen in the eyes of those that call
To make all that should be killed, to crawl
While others say, don't hate nothin' at all
Except hatred

Disillusioned words like bullets bark
As human Gods aim for their mark
Made everything from toy guns that spark
To flesh colored Christs that glow in the dark
It's easy to see without lookin' too far
That not much,
Is really sacred

While preachers preach of evil fates
Teachers teach that knowledge waits
Can lead to hundred dollar plates
Goodness hides behind its gates
But even the president of the United States
Sometimes must have
To stand naked
And though the rules of the road, have been lodged
It's only peoples games that you got to dodge
And it's alright ma, I can make it.

3. Advertising signs that con you
Into thinking you're the one
That can do what's never been done
That can win, what's never been won
Meantime life outside goes on
All around you

You lose yourself, you reappear
You suddenly find you got nothin' to fear
Alone you stand, with nobody near
When a trembling distant voice unclear
Startles your sleeping ears to hear
That somebody thinks
They really found you

A question in your nerves is lit
Yet you know there is no answer fit to satisfy.
Insure you not to quit
To keep it in your mind and not fergit
That it is not he or she or them or it
That you belong to
Although the masters make the rules
Of the wise men and the fools
I got nothing, ma
To live up to.

*4. For them that must obey authority
That they do not respect in any degree
Who despise their jobs, their destinies
Speak jealously of them that are free
Cultivate their flowers to be
Nothing more than something
They invest in

While some unprinciples baptized
To strict party platform ties
Social clubs in drag disguise
Outsiders achin' freely criticize
Tell nothin' except who to idolize
And say God bless him

While one who sings with his tongue on fire
Gargles in the rat race choir
Bent out of shape from society's pliers
Cares not to come up any higher
But rather get you down in the hole
That he's in
But I mean no harm, nor put fault
On anyone that lives in a vault
But it's alright ma, if I can please him

*5. Old lady judges watch people in pairs
Limited in sex, they dare
To push fake moral insult, and stare
While money doesn't talk, it swears
Obscenity, who really cares
Propaganda, all is phony

While them that defend what they cannot see
With a killer's pride, security
It blows the minds most bitterly
For them that think death's honesty
Won't fall upon them naturally
Life sometimes
Must get lonely

My eyes collide head on with stuffed graveyards,
False Gods, I scuff
At pettiness which plays so rough
Walk upside down inside handcuffs
Kick my legs to crash it off
Say okay, I've had enough
What else can you show me
And if my thought dreams could be seen
They'd probably put my head in a guillotine
But it's alright ma
It's life, and life only.

My Back Pages

Words and Music by Bob Dylan

1. Crim - son flames tied through my ears, Rol - lin'
2.-6. *See additional lyrics*

high and might - y traps, _____ Pounced with

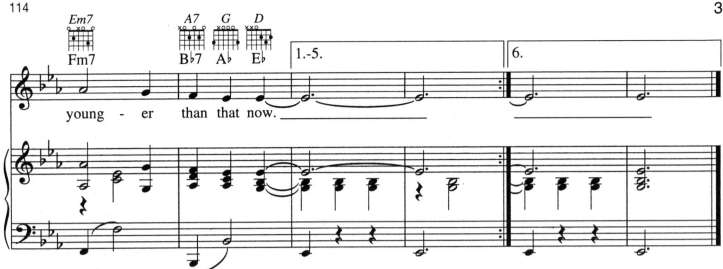

young - er than that now. _____

2. Half-wracked prejudice leaped forth,
   "Rip down all here," I screamed,
   Lies that life is black and white
   Spoke from my skull I dreamed.
   Romantic facts of musketeers,
   Foundationed deep, somehow,
   Ah, but I was so much older then,
   I'm younger than that now.

3. Girl's faces formed the forward path
   From phony jealousy,
   To memorizing politics
   Of ancient history.
   Flung down by corpse evangelist
   Unthought of, though, somehow,
   Ah, but I was so much older then,
   I'm younger than that now.

4. A self-ordained professor's tongue,
   Too serious to fool,
   Spouted out that liberty.
   Is just equality in school.
   "Equality," I spoke the word
   As if a wedding vow,
   Ah, but I was so much older then,
   I'm younger than that now.

5. In a soldier's stance I aimed my hand
   At the mongrel dogs who teach,
   Fearing not that I'd become my enemy
   In the instant that I preach.
   My pathway led by confusion boats,
   Mutiny from stern to bow,
   Ah, but I was so much older then,
   I'm younger than that now.

6. Yes, my guards stood hard when abstract threats
   Too noble to neglect
   Deceived me into thinking
   I had something to protect.
   Good and bad, I define these terms
   Quite clear, no doubt, somehow,
   Ah, but I was so much older then,
   I'm younger than that, now.

The 30th Anniversary Concert Celebration

Knockin' On Heaven's Door

Words and Music by Bob Dylan

Girl Of The North Country

Words and Music by Bob Dylan

Additional Lyrics

2. Well if you go in the snowflake storm
When the rivers freeze and summer ends,
Please see she has a coat so warm
To keep her from the howlin' winds.

3. Please see for me if her hair hangs long,
If it rolls and flows all down her breast,
Please see for me if her hair hangs long,
That's the way I remember her best.

4. I'm a-wonderin' if she remembers me at all,
Many times I've often prayed
In the darkness of my night,
In the brightness of my day,

5. So if you're trav'lin' in the north country fair,
Where the winds hit heavy on the borderline,
Remember me to one who lives there,
She once was a true love of mine.

The 30th Anniversary Concert Celebration